LEAD
YOURSELF
LEAD OTHERS

BY PHIL GELDART

EAGLE'S
FLIGHT™
experience. learning. impact.

Copyright © 2012
Eagle's Flight, Creative Training Excellence Inc.
ISBN 978-0-9685677-4-6

Printed in Canada

*To Roz, with thanks for her
unwavering support of my
own leadership journey.*

About the Title

Lead Yourself, Lead Others

I believe that our character drives our leadership effectiveness. Great leadership is not about trying to be what we're not; rather it's about helping others be the best they can be; for that, we must be the best that we can be.

From this flows the need for each of us to strive for personal mastery in several areas. As one acquires capability and confidence – that is, first leading ourselves – we can then lead others to a similar mastery, and so greater personal performance.

In this book I've outlined those key areas that I feel are crucial to our success and character as individuals, and consequently crucial for us as leaders to model, and teach.

As these become part of the fabric of our own lives we grow stronger and more effective. As we assume positions of leadership we can then pass these strengths on to those who are looking to us for direction, guidance, and growth.

I trust you will find these thoughts helpful on your own leadership journey.

Phil Geldart

Contents

Contents

Contents

Act Collaboratively

Leadership

Followership

Communication

Have Vision

Goals

Commitment

LEADERSHIP

A group is most successful working together when a leader has been identified whom the group agrees to follow.

Within every group, someone needs to be identified to lead.

1. Always, every time, identify a leader. The leader will be the final decision maker.

2. The individual chosen to lead does not always have to be the same person; in fact, if the requisite leadership skill is in place, have the leadership be taken by the person most familiar with what the group is trying to accomplish.

3. The leader's responsibilities include:

   • Making sure everyone knows what they've come together to accomplish

   • Ensuring everyone gets a chance to have their ideas and thoughts heard

   • Assigning tasks (if appropriate)

   • Taking responsibility to ensure the group does what it sets out to do

4. Sometimes, large projects can be broken into smaller projects, each with its own leader.

LEADERSHIP

When groups are working together to achieve something specific, they can be far more effective when there's an identified leader. The leader can take responsibility for deciding when it's time to move from discussion to action; for making a final decision from among several options if there's not one immediately obvious to everybody; for helping to ensure that everyone has a chance to present their point of view; and to make sure the discussion stays on topic.

The leadership role is very important because it identifies one individual in the group whose responsibility it is to guide, or shepherd, the group along the path from where they began to where they want to finish up. It's important for everyone to recognize that this does not mean that the leader dominates and has the right to simply impose their will. The leader's job is to ensure that the group comes together so the best decision can be made using everyone's input.

Every team needs a designated leader, and the leader carries responsibility for the team's final outcome. The leader must ensure that the team functions effectively, stays focused on its goal, and delivers its mandate. While the leader carries the final responsibility to ensure the mandate is in fact achieved, the members of the team have the responsibility to support the leader in the achievement of that objective.

Always identify a leader and then be willing to personally support that person's leadership.

Identify the Leader

FOLLOWERSHIP

A group can only collaborate when everyone is willing to work together, following the leader to produce the agreed outcome.

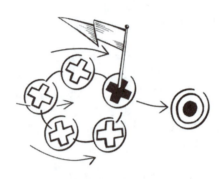

**Being committed to following the leader
promotes collaboration.**

1. It's difficult to be a good leader until you've been a good follower.

2. Groups collaborating together must be made up of individuals who are working hard to be good followers.

3. A group with good followers is unified, focused, and productive.

4. A good follower is one who:
   - Voices honest opinions
   - Contributes to discussions
   - Publicly and privately fully supports the leader's final decision
   - Says in private only what they would also say in public
   - Works wholeheartedly, consistently, and enthusiastically to achieve the group's goals

FOLLOWERSHIP

Sometimes it appears easier to be the leader than to be the follower. As the leader, you are the one to make the final decision; however, to be a good leader you must first know how to be a good follower. This requires learning to listen to your leader, and being willing to throw yourself completely behind the final decision made on behalf of the group.

If you have a group of people where everybody wants to be the leader, or is acting as the leader, then it is very hard for the group to be collaborative. They end up with each person pulling in their own direction; the group generally becomes frustrated and goes nowhere. However, simply identifying the leader doesn't help if everybody else isn't willing to then follow appropriately.

Following does not mean blindly doing what you're told. Rather, it means recognizing that when the leader has to exert the authority of their position to make a decision, or provide direction, you as the follower are willing to follow that direction and trust your leader's ability. Learning to be a good follower is great training for learning to be a good leader.

On a team, each member is responsible to work together for the benefit of the group. There is no place for individual egos to dominate; rather, each person on the team needs to understand that they are there to support the whole, under the direction of the leader. The whole is truly greater than the sum of the parts, and each of the individual parts must recognize that they are there to serve the whole and not their own interests. This attitude on the part of each team member is essential to the team's success.

The biggest challenge to being a good follower is when the leader and group have decided on a direction that's different from your preference. That is also the biggest opportunity to demonstrate good followership.

A good follower is wind in the group's sails!

COMMUNICATION

Each person must take personal responsibility to ensure every relationship they have is rooted in strong communication.

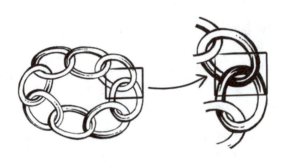

The secret to strong links is strong two-way communication.

1. A group working collaboratively is like a chain linked together, and communication occurs where they link. If the communication is weak, the link is weak and the chain will break.

2. Strong communication means:
   - It's two-way; both people listen without interrupting, and both speak their mind
   - It's honest, and not half-truths
   - It's done with consideration and respect for the other person
   - It's based on fact, not ego, personality, or "winning points"

3. Collaborating requires a "meeting of the minds." Rarely do all the minds start out at the same place; communication is what brings them together. The better the communication, the stronger the collaboration.

COMMUNICATION

Communication is certainly a vital issue within any group, and unless every member is really working hard to ensure good communication, it tends to break down and fall apart.

Good communication is everyone's responsibility, and while the leader may be nudging individuals within the group to improve their communication, it is still each individual's responsibility to communicate as well as possible.

Very often words have different meanings to different people, so even group members who are well-intentioned do not necessarily communicate as effectively as they would like without working hard at it. Working at communication ensures that there are no misunderstandings, no misinterpretations, and time is spent productively, instead of bickering or rehashing topics that have become unclear simply because of poor communication.

Communication within a team is the responsibility of all the members. It is the leader's responsibility to ensure that communication is effective and frequent. It is each team member's responsibility to do everything possible to speak with clarity, and provide all the necessary information available when questions or issues arise needing their input. Each individual needs to understand that they carry the responsibility to ensure that the other individuals on the team have all the information they need in order to be as successful as possible.

A strong chain can be very powerful. Strong individual pieces are important, but for maximum strength, the pieces must also be effectively joined. This requires everyone to become strong at communication.

**Progressively strengthen each link
through great communication.**

HAVE VISION

The vision behind your actions is like folklore; it grows richer and more powerful with each retelling. Keep the vision alive.

Each group needs to have a vision they're working towards, the "why" for their activity.

1. People will collaborate most effectively when they know why they need to do so. They want to be able to mentally picture the outcome.

2. A vision is accomplished by achieving objectives, or agreed upon outcomes. Objectives are steps to the vision and so very important, but they are not the vision itself.

3. Visions are intangible and usually hard to really define or write down. They're usually more easily conceptualized than articulated.

4. But once shared, understood, and agreed to, they provide the motivation to begin to work together, set objectives, and truly become collaborative to make the vision a reality.

HAVE VISION

It's much more exciting when the group has a vision that they're working towards. This provides energy, enthusiasm, anticipation, and motivation for the group to work hard to see the vision come to pass. Each person needs to spend time to really understand the vision, and why it's important to them.

Visions are usually motivating and should be the foundation for most significant action.

The team's vision, the statement of its reason to be, defines why the team was initiated in the first place, and articulates the big picture statement of what the team is committed to achieving. It needs to create passion, excitement, and enthusiasm in its members, and reinforce for them why it is they are working so hard together.

Visions drive actions. Share them. Refine them. Understand them, then work together to see them materialize.

**Take time to remember why you're
doing something. When the vision is alive,
the group is engaged and energized.**

GOALS

*A series of clear, universally understood goals
is what gives the group its focus for action when together,
and confidence their vision is achievable.*

Before beginning, know exactly what you want to achieve.

1. The best way to make sure everyone in the group knows what they're working together on is to:

   • Discuss it together

   • Answer any "I don't understand" questions

   • Write out the desired outcome

2. Write out the steps necessary to achieve that outcome in the form of goals.

3. It may seem unnecessary to write this out, but doing so ensures:

   • Everyone can check it whenever they need to and be reminded of the focus

   • Everyone, for sure, now has the same understanding

   • Fuzzy or assumed pieces get clarified

4. Once the goals are written down, use them to see how you're doing as you work towards your desired outcome, and as a final check to see if you've achieved it.

GOALS

A vision can only become reality when there are a series of steps to get you there from where you are now. The vision is extremely important because it provides direction; the steps are also extremely important because they provide the specific action that you will take to see that vision come to pass.

After the vision is clear, then you need to decide what specific steps you will be taking, phrased as action-oriented goals or objectives. There could be five or twenty-five steps that have to be taken before the vision can be realized. The steps then become your focus.

The realization of the vision only comes as a result of the rigorous discipline of doing each individual step well, and in sequence.

As each goal is achieved, then move on to the next, knowing that the cumulative achievement of each of these goals in sequence will allow realization of the vision. As such, these goals need to be clear, actionable, measurable, and specifically spelled out. The goal itself may not engender passion, but its achievement reinforces the conviction that the next goal is obtainable and, ultimately, so is the vision. Goals play an important part for each team in that they provide immediate focus for their action.

Everyone agreeing to a written statement of what you're about to do ensures all the rowers are rowing the boat in the same direction.

**Everyone needs to concentrate
on the same objective.**

COMMITMENT

*Personally bring your full commitment to bear,
and expect others to do so as well.*

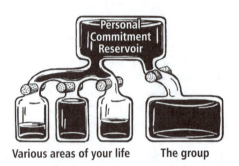

Various areas of your life   The group

The group requires you to be fully committed to the agreed outcome.

1. There are several areas of life demanding your personal commitment. Some require you to be fully committed (e.g., marriage) and some only partially (e.g., a hobby).

2. For a group to be as effective as possible, all members need to be fully committed to the agreed outcome when they're working on behalf of the group.

3. Being fully committed manifests itself as follows:

   • Sharing personal resources with the group (as appropriate)

   • Giving your 100% effort all the time

   • Showing initiative

   • Recognizing, and acting as if, the group will not succeed without you

   • Being supportive of one another – in challenging times and triumphant ones

COMMITMENT

Once the decision has been made on the direction to be taken, and the steps to follow identified, each individual has to be fully committed to deliver against those steps. Very often, each step requires help from other members of the group, and if you are unwilling to give your wholehearted support, then that step won't be accomplished on time or as intended. Each individual plays an important role in seeing the overall vision come to pass.

Commitment requires enthusiasm. When you're doing what it is you said you would do, it must be clear that you are fully committed to it, and not doing it grudgingly or unwillingly. If this enthusiasm is not displayed, then others tend to feel annoyed that wholehearted effort is not being given, which in turn has the consequence of generally detracting from the work at hand.

Each team member has to be fully committed to the achievement of each of the goals, and ultimately the realization of the vision. This full commitment means that they remain unanimous, working together; they do not allow other objectives to sidetrack them from their task; they remain consistent in their effort, not sometimes "hot" and sometimes "cold" in their efforts; and they constantly bring their enthusiasm to bear. This represents commitment to the team's objectives on the part of each individual.

Full collaboration requires full commitment. Anything less diminishes the group's effectiveness, and so impacts the finished product.

Not this...   **This!**

 but...

The whole cannot work well without each part being fully involved.

Keep Improving Yourself

Learn New Skills

Postmortem

Be Patient

Learning Mindset

Self Control

Apply It

LEARN NEW SKILLS

Collect and fill personal skill jars.

Imagine a pantry shelf with several jars.

1. Imagine pantry shelves with jars of different sizes filled to different levels, with different ingredients.

2. Each jar represents a skill, either generic (like listening), or functional (like interviewing).

3. How full it is represents how much of that skill you have.

4. "Full" means "highly skilled."

Jar = Skill

Level = How skilled you are

5. Over time, try to:

   • Fill the jars you now have

   • Add more jars; start by listing the skills you'd like to have, and then work at adding more

LEARN NEW SKILLS

When you learn new skills, it is an investment in yourself. New skills allow you to do new things, tackle old things from a new perspective, and get better results. They give you the ability to deal with issues more effectively, or in a way that you never used to be able to do.

The greater your skill set, the more options you have in terms of how to approach an issue or situation, or use your time. Also, as you constantly learn new things, you keep your mental faculties sharp, and your flexibility and willingness to look at new things (or old things in a different way) functioning in high gear.

You may wish to learn tangible skills, like making presentations, managing projects, or writing a strategic plan. You may wish to consider intangible skills such as becoming a better listener, becoming more persuasive, or being more assertive. You could also consider taking courses from a university or community college.

Individuals bring to the organization their skill sets, as well as their commitment and dedication. As their skills are enhanced, so is their value to the organization and their ability to do their job more effectively. The stronger the person, the stronger the outcome which they can produce. Constantly investing in and improving your skills is an extremely effective way to contribute to the performance of the organization of which you are a part, as well as your own personal satisfaction and job competence.

The more highly skilled you are, the better you'll be able to deal with people, issues, and opportunities that come your way.

Collect and fill several personal skill jars!

POSTMORTEM

*Learn from looking backwards
to find ways to do it better next time.*

After you're done, take a moment to consider how you did it.

This is a "postmortem." Once the task is completely done — "in a box with a bow on it" — take a few minutes and ask:

1. Could I have done it better?

2. Could I have done it faster?

3. Could I have done it cheaper?

4. If so…how?

POSTMORTEM

A great way to continue to improve yourself is to set aside time after something has been completed, and review it to see what you can learn from the experience. This "postmortem" is effective both after you've done something simple, and after a major activity or project has been completed.

It's true that we learn best by our experience, but unless we pause after each experience and consider how we can apply our learning the next time, then we're not really learning from the experience; we're just having the experience. It takes some mental discipline to pause after something is done and review what's been learned, rather than going on to the next task, especially if the next task is interesting or exciting. However, time spent on a postmortem is a great way to improve your skills.

Very often a postmortem is best when it's done together with others who have also been involved in the task or project with you.

Given the power of experience as a learning vehicle, and the frequency with which some tasks are repeated month to month and year to year, all completed activities of any significance would benefit from a postmortem. Analysis of what was done well, and what could be done better in the next cycle, produces significant learning based on experience and practicality. Scheduling a postmortem review upon completion of each significant task provides a major opportunity for ongoing improvement of performance.

**Don't move forward until
you've looked back!**

BE PATIENT

Improvement takes time. Be patient!

Grass seed takes a while to grow...
but ultimately you get a lawn!

1. Planting seeds with the intention of getting a nice, green lawn means you know you'll have to wait.

2. Then, if there's sun and water, you see the little blades become a beautiful lawn.

3. When you, or someone else, is working at learning something new...give it time to happen.

BE PATIENT

In a world of microwave ovens, internet fiber optics, and immediate coverage of world events, we tend to want everything to occur instantly or, if not instantly, certainly in a matter of seconds. If we have to wait too long even for a phone to be answered, we tend to get impatient, expecting that things should happen more and more quickly. However, self improvement is more like taking a trip than surfing the internet. It takes time.

As a result, you need to be patient with yourself and with others as you begin to learn new skills and work at self improvement. "How-to" skills come more quickly, like learning to use new software or a new company process. The more intangible ones like listening skills and communication skills tend to take more time, more practice, and require more patience to learn and master.

It is sometimes much easier to be patient with ourselves than to be patient with others. We forget that others also need the same time to make the journey of self improvement. We need to remember this and so manage both our own expectations and theirs, recognizing that individual improvement requires patience. While the results from personal development are often wanted as quickly as possible, the growth that occurs in individuals takes time, and we need to be patient and allow that growth to occur. Insights need to be tested, experience needs to be incorporated, and learning needs to be integrated with existing procedures. Being patient and allowing this process to occur over time produces long-term, sustained results.

The soil = individual willingness to improve
The seed = the new knowledge
The little shoots = some new skill
Water = help, coaching, advice
Sun = encouragement
The lawn = ultimate success!

**Growing action from learning
takes time. Be patient!**

LEARNING MINDSET

*Be committed to the premeditated learning
of new skills and approaches.*

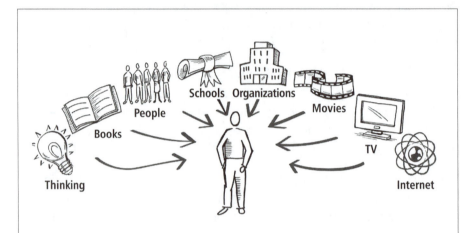

Schools Organizations
People Movies
Books TV
Thinking Internet

Have a state of mind that looks to learn.

1. There are many places to learn from, but actually learning something from them needs to be a conscious decision.

2. Wishing and wanting and intending don't count. Set aside specific time and energy to focus on learning.

3. "Premeditated" = planned in advance. Personal improvement learning must be premeditated!

LEARNING MINDSET

One of the exciting things about being committed to self improvement is the opportunity to learn from many different sources. We don't always have to go to a course, a class, or a college to learn things. There are lots of opportunities around us. One of the best ways to learn is from one another.

In addition, most of us have a lot of opportunity to connect with other groups or associations, colleagues at work, friends, or relatives who also have different skills and knowledge and from whom we could learn. If we have a learner's heart, then we will see each of these opportunities as a chance to acquire new skills by watching others, seeing how they do it, and then trying the skill for ourselves.

In sports, one of the best ways to learn is to watch someone better than us, and then try to copy what they are doing. The same applies to our day-to-day business lives.

The important thing is that we go into events or experiences with a predetermined, committed, and open-minded approach to learning.

Success in and of itself can often be a detriment, in that it can keep us from looking for new ways to do things (unlike failure, which drives us to look for alternate approaches!) Within any organization, each individual needs to have a high degree of commitment to personal development, and a mindset that values personal growth and improvement. Even the most successful can be even more so by learning to do it faster or better or more economically. As they increase in their own learning or skill, they set the pace for others within the organization.

Know what you want to learn – or learn more about – and find a source of information. Then, go get it, and absorb it.

Be committed to premeditated learning.

SELF CONTROL

The impact you have on others is at its maximum when you have your own self fully under control.

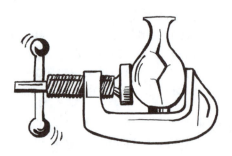

Master self control – always be sensitive to the circumstances.

1. Adjusting the pressure on a vise used to hold a broken, fragile pot requires a careful, sensitive touch. You need to be cautious, yet decisive; sensitive yet effective.

2. So, in life, your words and actions are like a vise; they can crush and destroy, or gently hold and support.

3. Learning to use them to achieve the desired end is called "self control," and it's something we need to be continuously improving.

4. Two of the best ways to achieve good self control are:

   • Think how you'd like to behave – and then strive for that

   • Do a postmortem after an unsuccessful attempt and learn from that

SELF CONTROL

One specific area where we need to be constantly working at self improvement is our own self control. It may seem like a strange topic to work on under the category of self improvement, but self control is something at which we need to become extremely good, and as such justifies us putting a lot of energy and focus on improving it.

The need for self control can show up in a discussion with a family member, subordinate, peer, or supervisor. We may find ourselves saying something which we later regret, or acting in a way which, on later reflection, we feel was inappropriate. To avoid speaking or acting that way in the first place requires self control. In this case, self control means to first ask yourself, "Am I about to say or do something which is hurtful, inappropriate, or that I'll later wish I hadn't said or done?" It's this kind of review before speaking or acting that requires great self control.

Despite our desire to behave in a certain way, we often find ourselves being "forced" into a different kind of behavior because circumstances seem to be conspiring against us. As a result, we become agitated or feel antagonized. In fact, we are not "forced" to act in any particular way; rather, we choose to let those circumstances direct our actions or behavior. As we work at improving our self control, it's a matter of ensuring that the choices we make are the ones which, upon reflection after the incident, we're glad we made rather than sorry we made.

Lack of self control, even for a moment, can often undo a great deal of good. Most organizations are looking for those who can demonstrate personal self control before they are willing to give them control of others, a complicated process, or a significant outcome. By demonstrating self control, we instill calm in others and confidence in our approach. This allows those around us to focus on the task at hand, not worrying about whether or not those with whom they're working, or perhaps following, are going to lose control.

Achieve the result you intended.

APPLY IT

New learning that's not used and applied is like you never learned those things in the first place.

Having oil and not using it is like not having it.

1. As you gain new learning, it must be applied to be of any value.

2. An engine can't function if oil is available but not used. The oil has to be added as a conscious act, deliberately done.

3. So you must consciously determine to apply newly learned skills and understanding. This takes some extra time and effort, but it's the only way to produce real improvement.

APPLY IT

There's a big difference between knowing intellectually what was taught at a course on creating stained glass windows, and actually going home and making one – learning how what was taught actually works in practice. When you begin to apply what was taught, you learn what was meant.

This same principle is true with everything that you learn in the hopes of acquiring new skills – if you don't apply the skills, it's really like never having learned them at all.

This is particularly difficult when you're trying to learn intangible or "soft" skills like communication, more so than it is for more tangible things, like learning to use a forklift. When we get into the intangible areas, it always seems easier to go back to the previous way. We may recognize that it is not as effective as we would like, but typically at that moment we're "too busy" to try to apply a new skill. And what's sometimes even worse, when we do apply it, we feel as though we are even less effective than we were with the old skills. That's because, like anything new, it takes time to really get the hang of it and get good at it. Only by persevering and consistently working at applying each new skill will you get the benefit and see the value.

The application of learning is crucial and requires self discipline. The acquisition of learning about new skills is easy. However, the application of that learning requires focus, time, and an intense commitment of our will to ensure that we actually apply what we have learned.

As you acquire new skills, make a point of using them until you see a change in yourself.

Deliver What You Promise

Crystal Clear

Agreement

Available Freedom

Consequences

Hierarchy of Action

Executional Excellence

CRYSTAL CLEAR

*Ensure you provide clarity around expectations,
and then ensure you deliver the expected results.*

An unclear view   A crystal clear view

What you promise must be absolutely crystal clear to others.

1. It's not only what you mean to do, it's also what others think you mean to do.

2. It's not what you think you've told others you'll do; it's knowing for sure exactly what they expect.

3. Make sure there's perfect clarity on the expected, or promised, outcome.

4. Get this clarity in advance.

CRYSTAL CLEAR

We always know exactly what we mean. We're very clear in our mind about what we intend to do, and by when, and how we intend to do it. However, it's another matter altogether to give others that same degree of understanding.

Often other people hear our words through their own filters, through whatever is most important to them at the moment. Consequently, they hear what we say not as we intended but rather as they would like to hear it, or as they think we should have said it. This can lead to confusion and also to people making wrong judgements. You may judge me badly because I didn't do what you thought I was going to do. I then judge you badly for the way you responded, because I did exactly what I said I would do, not realizing it was different from what you thought I was going to do.

When making commitments to others, take a few extra minutes to get accurate clarification, to ensure you both understand the same thing.

Individuals who have made commitments are accountable for those commitments, and that should mean there is an absolute guarantee that what has been promised will be delivered. The first step in the process of accountability is for both parties to be crystal clear on what is expected and what will be delivered. This is not the time for assumptions, or leaving things implied or unspoken. When committing to deliver a result, or asking for one, be absolutely certain that there is specific, detailed, unanimous clarity regarding the finished product. This ensures mutual understanding, and no surprises!

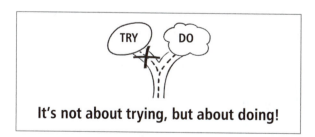

It's not about trying, but about doing!

AGREEMENT

Get agreement before action if you want the promise
to come with a guarantee.

Make sure there's up-front agreement
to deliver an outcome. Don't just assign it.

1. If the person who's expected to deliver something (an action, a result, a behavior) doesn't agree to deliver it, then there's a possible problem.

2. The "receiver" expects to get it, but the "provider" may feel that:

   • It's not practical

   • There's not enough time (or money, space, resources, or freedom) to deliver it

   • It conflicts with other priorities

   • The request is unreasonable

3. If one of these situations is the case, it's better to know it in advance, so you can work it out together.

4. "Working it out together" means discussing it through until you've agreed on what and when. Only then does it become a promise that can be counted on.

AGREEMENT

Sometimes we are able to "wring" a promise out of someone. Essentially, this is when we are so convinced that our way is correct that we either impose, cajole, or sometimes browbeat the other person into making some form of a commitment. We are so convinced that our approach is right that we want them to act on the basis of our convictions!

As a result, the person will "promise" to deliver something when really they either believe it's not practical, or it's not something they will put too much effort into because they themselves are not as committed to it as you are, or as you want them to be. You need to be sensitive to this and careful that you do not let it occur, either by letting others do it to you, or by you doing it to others. It is very important that both parties walk away with a real sense of agreement and understanding of what they've agreed to as a basis for a promised outcome.

Having this kind of understanding and agreement, that both people are equally committed to, is crucial to ensuring success.

Simply assigning an absolutely crystal clear mandate to an individual, and then walking away assuming that mandate will be fulfilled, is not consistent with defining accountabilities. For that mandate to be fulfilled, the individual receiving it must agree to it, and agree that it is in fact doable. Without this agreement, you do not have the confidence that it will be delivered as expected. Whatever discussion is necessary must occur before any action begins. Once the commitments have been agreed to, then the individual delivering can be held accountable for the results.

Discuss, agree, get commitment. It's only a promise you can count on when both "giver" and "provider" have agreed in advance.

Guarantee

Based on agreement.

AVAILABLE FREEDOM

*Know what freedom you have,
or are giving, to deliver on a promise.*

**The size of the paddock determines
the scope of the stallion's freedom.**

1. When assigning responsibilities to others, or taking them on yourself, make sure to explain, or get clarity, on the size of the paddock.

2. The size of a person's promise must be in balance with the size of the paddock. Some good questions to use for this are:

   • How much "freedom" (time, space, resources, advice) is needed to ensure the success of this promise?

   • Where are the boundaries, or limits, for this assignment or promise? Does everyone agree on these? (Limits can be with respect to time, money, use of things, and decisions)

AVAILABLE FREEDOM

Typically, when we have made a commitment to deliver something, we have a degree of freedom available to us in order to fulfill that commitment. This freedom can be how long we have to do the job, how much money we can spend, what other resources we can pull in, how often we need to report in, etc. Whenever we assign this kind of freedom to somebody else, or are given it ourselves, we need to be confident that the amount of freedom we have to do the job is sufficient to ensure the job gets done.

When we don't have enough freedom, doing the job becomes very difficult, and sometimes impossible. On the other hand, if we have too much freedom, then there's a chance of making a large mistake, or misusing a significant amount of the resources available. Matching the freedom to the job ensures that there is a much greater chance of success. Consequently, the available freedom is very important and needs to be well spelled out and understood by all concerned.

When an individual is given accountability, they also need to be given the scope within which they have to act. This scope should spell out the resources they have to work with as well as the decision-making parameters. Without spelling out the degree of freedom, both parties may move down the path towards accomplishment based on different assumptions. As a result, the agreed outcome will likely not materialize. To avoid this, ensure both parties are clear on what is the scope for the person with the task, before it's initiated.

Know the paddock size and make sure everyone agrees on that size before action is taken to deliver on the promise.

All must know and agree on the paddock size.

CONSEQUENCES

Know in advance the consequences of successfully and unsuccessfully delivering on your promise.

Done as promised **Not done as promised**

There must be consequences for both success and failure.

1. Ensure there's understanding in advance regarding the nature of consequences – both for success and failure.

2. Consequences should be aligned with impact. Big impact – significant consequences (whether the promise is delivered or not). Small impact – minor consequences.

3. "Impact" can be on something (e.g., a project), or character (e.g., honesty), or somebody (e.g., a customer), or a plan (e.g., "We need that done before we can do this").

4. "Consequences" can range from something said ("Well done") all the way through to something done ("How does a week at a resort sound?").

CONSEQUENCES

Being responsible includes accepting the consequences of our actions. To ensure responsible behavior, we must also ensure that there are consequences as a result of that behavior.

When an individual makes a promise to do something, and is successful at it, then there should be the naturally occurring consequences of the promise itself being delivered. Additional positive consequences may be: praise, allowing a greater degree of personal freedom, taking on of greater responsibility, or the ability to have a greater influence on subsequent decisions.

Similarly, when promises are not met, there needs to be negative consequences as a result. These could include less responsibility in the future, not allowing further action until the initial promise is completed, restriction of the freedom to act by requiring additional direction, or some form of rebuke. Having consequences keeps the promises from being hollow.

With accountability goes responsibility, and as a result, the accountable individual must bear the final responsibility for the results. On a team, results are owned by the leader; for individual assignments, results are owned by the individual. Bearing the responsibility means that the individual must accept the consequences of failure, or less than complete success; these need to be spelled out in advance, and then adhered to. Similarly, the consequences of success also need to be spelled out and adhered to. Without consequences, the focus on accountability is hollow.

A promise is something on which others depend, and on which our personal integrity sits. As such, consequences for success or failure go with the territory.

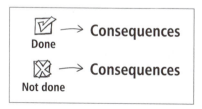

HIERARCHY OF ACTION

*Make your promises based on delivery
to the most important people or things first.*

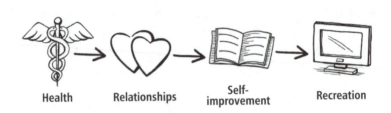

Health   Relationships   Self-improvement   Recreation

Make promises according to a predetermined sequence or hierarchy.

1. Who the promise is made to often determines whether or not you can, or should, make the promise at all — since there's rarely enough time to do everything.

2. The priority sequence you establish for your promises should focus on putting those people or things at the front that are the most important.

3. An example might be:

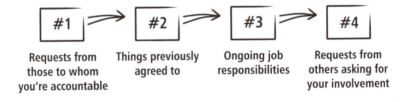

#1 Requests from those to whom you're accountable

#2 Things previously agreed to

#3 Ongoing job responsibilities

#4 Requests from others asking for your involvement

4. The order in which you do things should mirror the same sequence you used when making your promises. In this way, you're always putting your energy behind the most crucial promises, and by so doing ensuring that you always deliver on the most important things.

HIERARCHY OF ACTION

Since delivering on what we promise is so important, it makes sense to know which things should be given the highest priority. To deliver on a relatively unimportant promise at the expense of a really crucial one neither makes sense nor is it the best use of time.

Consequently, those involved need to sit together and determine what the major priorities are, and put them into some form of rank order. In this way, it's much easier to make a decision on what to leave undone in the event you can't get everything done that you had hoped to do. At least you'll be able to ensure that the most crucial promises are delivered.

Accountabilities need to be hierarchically organized. This hierarchy needs to be clearly spelled out in advance so that the individual knows what can be compromised and what cannot. Having this hierarchy also allows you to determine when you can make a commitment to be accountable for something and when you can't. For example, if customers are an absolute priority in your organization, and you've made a commitment to a customer that takes a great deal of time to fulfill, you may not be able to make an equally large commitment to someone within the organization, because you know there is not the time to deliver both. In this case you've placed the customer's needs above those of someone in your organization. Defining this hierarchy is based on judgment, and needs to be established in advance in order to allow you to decide what you can and cannot commit to.

A promise made must be kept and delivered. Make sure the most important promises are therefore considered first!

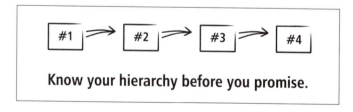

Know your hierarchy before you promise.

EXECUTIONAL EXCELLENCE

Making the promise is only the first step – delivering it then requires identifying everything that must be done, followed by dotting all the i's and crossing all the t's.

Deliver on your promise as predictably and reliably as a Swiss watch tells time.

1. The key to successfully delivering on your promises is to pay attention to:

   • Everything that needs to be done

   • The details that must be included

2. Simply making a well-intentioned promise does not guarantee the result.

3. List everything that must be completed to deliver on the promise, and then methodically work through the list – even if sometimes it's boring, or you're tempted to cut corners. Do it all, and do it well.

4. Also, when you're doing something on the list, stick with it until each detail is addressed. That way, nothing is overlooked, the result is rock solid, and can be delivered with pride.

EXECUTIONAL EXCELLENCE

If we make a promise to deliver on an outcome, then at that moment in time we are committing to seeing it through and delivering on it. We have the very best of intentions and are determined to persevere. This is good and important, but is still only the first step. We need to follow up on that desire with a lot of concrete action.

When we get to the action steps, very often we have to do them when we are tired, when we would rather be doing something else, or getting pressure from other priorities. It's at this point that "the rubber meets the road" and we must make the decisions required to deliver on what we've already committed.

One of the best ways to make sure we actually follow through on our promises, is to make the plan right after we make the promise, and then stick to the plan knowing that after we've finished all the steps, the promise will have been fulfilled. If we just try to "wing it" from day to day, then very often the pressures or urgencies of the moment can work to pull us off our intentions, and we fail to deliver on what we've promised. A real commitment to detailed, specific, preplanned action must follow a promise if there is to be any hope of that promise being fulfilled.

Long-term credibility is only gained by the consistent long-term delivering on our accountabilities. In order to ensure this consistent delivery, our focus needs to be on executional excellence. Develop a detailed and specific plan that will give you the confidence that, if followed, will ensure you deliver the promised outcome. Leave nothing to chance, no "bridges that will be crossed when you get there." Rather, give considerable thought to the details of the execution. Do not end the planning process until you're confident that you have a thorough plan, one you can be committed to following, knowing that success will follow if you execute it fully.

Know and deliver on the detail.

Maintain Balance

Family vs. Work

Self vs. Group

Urgent vs. Important

Pride vs. Humility

Good vs. Great

Influenced vs. Independent

FAMILY VS. WORK

Ensure you have the right balance today. All your tomorrows are only a collection of todays, so today being in balance is important.

**Ensure time spent on home and family
is in balance with time spent at work.**

1. Work is clearly very important – it provides income, some stability, opportunity for personal growth, and a measure of security. As such, it deserves your best efforts, always.

2. However, home, and the issues that surround home, are also vital. Relatives, parents, friends, spouse, children, hobbies, leisure, community involvement, and faith all contribute to providing personal balance and perspective.

3. Often, work issues are immediate and pressing, while home issues can be more easily postponed (the "urgent" – work, compared to the "important" – home). Recognize this and avoid falling into the trap of "I'll put off the home things, just for now." That time is never recovered.

4. Both work and home are important, but keeping the balance of time spent on each where it should be (which is not necessarily 50/50) is more important. If you want to know if the balance is moving away from equilibrium, ask for input from all those involved – their opinion is a valuable way to help you stay balanced.

FAMILY VS. WORK

When we think of balance around our working lives, we tend to think very much in the short term, that is, "Am I working too many hours this week?" or "Should I be at home?" or conversely "Should I be putting in more hours at work to get things done there sooner?" Clearly the short-term view is important, and one which needs a lot of consideration.

However, very often the issue is not as simple as that. Work issues may be very demanding, or perhaps there are some issues at home requiring your extended attention. In these situations, the issue is less about maintaining balance week to week and more about achieving balance over the longer term.

The important thing to realize is that if you have to spend extended hours at home, or at work, for a period of time, that you do not let that become the normal behavior, which will then result in your work/family balance being inappropriate. Do what you need to do in either area for as long as you need to do it, but not on an ongoing basis. At the end of every year, you should be able to look back and feel that the books are appropriately balanced between work and family.

It's important to maintain balance between work and family, not only for the sake of your own mental well-being, but also because of the example that you set for those around you. Further, we are each dependent on the intangible support we receive from those at home, and it is crucial to ensure that we invest as significantly at home as we do at work. It's difficult to be fully focused on the job at hand when there are problems at home, perhaps because you've neglected the balance between work and family. Similarly, the organization has the right to expect both your time and a high degree of performance in exchange for the compensation they provide. Take personal control of this balance, rather than letting circumstances control you.

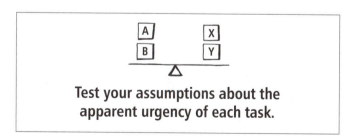

Test your assumptions about the apparent urgency of each task.

SELF VS. GROUP

Invest time keeping yourself strong and at your peak.
This is best for all those you interact with, and ensures
you can always keep contributing to your fullest.

Invest time and energy in yourself as well as in the group.

1. Your contributions to the groups of which you are a part are vital. They need you and want you. As such, it's often easy to find ourselves continually "giving our all," whether the group is our family, a volunteer committee, or at work.

2. At times, this can be extremely draining, and we feel "bone weary" or "worn out" or "just have nothing more to give." This is not healthy for you, or the group to which you're so committed.

3. Before getting to that "totally drained" stage, invest time in yourself. This does not mean becoming egocentric and selfish; rather, it means setting aside regular and frequent time to do what you need to do to keep your personal batteries charged.

4. This may mean going for a run each day, soaking in a hot tub in the evening, attending a night course, or taking periodic weekends off to shop, read, sleep, visit, or see a play.

5. The important thing is not what you do, but that you do it on a consistent basis — that you balance your investment in yourself with your investment in others.

SELF VS. GROUP

You bring to your responsibilities all the things that make you unique and special. Your contributions are vital regardless of your role in the group with which you're associated. You are there because they need you and want you. Your contributions move things ahead and make the environment richer for all concerned.

As a result, you need to be careful to ensure that whatever it is that you need to do for you, to keep your own "inner sanity," you do. You must recognize that it's a priority to balance your time against the contributions you make to the family and the groups with which you are associated, and the time and the energy you spend on yourself. For example, if you feel you need some quiet time to yourself and the best time to get it is in the morning, then schedule your time and the activities of your life around getting the time that you need in the morning. Alternatively, you may enjoy a game of tennis as a way of recharging your batteries and staying fit, and this may be best done in the evening. In this case, ensure that you get that relaxation and recharging at the end of the day.

One danger is that in an effort to "recharge," individuals actually neglect their responsibilities to the family or the groups with which they are associated, under the guise of "I deserve a break" or "I deserve recharge time." Too much focus on self is as bad as too little. However, some time for yourself each day is crucial to ensuring that you are always able to give your very best to those who depend on you.

Make yourself a priority in your own planning – and keep to that priority.

**The group always benefits from
a stronger you.**

URGENT VS. IMPORTANT

Spend a few minutes determining if your energy is being wisely spent, maintaining the proper balance between the urgent and the important.

Urgent   Important

Balance the need to "fight fires" with the need to "build firewalls."

1. **"Urgent"** — means it must be done right now or something very crucial isn't dealt with.

2. **"Important"** — means it must be done, or the longer term consequences will be very undesirable. It doesn't need doing today — just some day soon.

3. The nature of urgent things is such that they keep us from important things. But usually the urgent, once done, is quickly forgotten.

4. As you choose how to spend your time, create a balance between these two — spend the appropriate amount of time on each.

5. Practically, to help with this:
   • Ask yourself "What is the real impact of not doing this?"; it will tell you how crucial it is, or isn't, that you do it
   • Put some "important" time into creating ways to eliminate the things which cause the urgencies; then you'll have fewer of them

URGENT VS. IMPORTANT

"Urgent things" is one of the ways to look at our responsibilities. Urgent things are crucial and very much tend to drive our lives. The other way is to identify "important things." They tend to be next in line, because we know that if we don't do them they will become urgent, and we'll perhaps be obligated to do them at a time when we would prefer to do something else. Important things, such as regularly taking time for yourself, often seem to be easily put off. We feel there's always time for this later, because of the pressure to do the urgent things. Maintain balance between the urgent and the important.

Urgent things are the day-to-day things which are typically short-term in focus and significant only within that time frame. On the other hand, the important things tend to have a longer-term outlook, and usually result in longer-term improvement. The important things tend to be things which will create long-term change, like improving efficiencies resulting in waste elimination. The important things typically minimize the number of urgent things. Do not neglect the important because of the tyranny of the urgent, but rather manage your time and resources to realize the potential of the important.

The more you spend time on important things, the fewer urgent things you'll have.

The issue to bear in mind is not that the urgent is bad and the important is good, or vice versa, but rather that life needs to be made up of an appropriate amount of each. Carefully sitting down to think through how much time should go against each, and what should be done during that time, will lead to the appropriate balance.

**Urgent is present. Important is future.
Invest in the future.**

PRIDE VS. HUMILITY

When you're successful, enhance that success in the eyes of others by demonstrating sincere humility and quiet pride.

Humility   What you've accomplished

Value your accomplishments, but also the larger perspective.

1. Succeeding, and achieving things, is wonderful and important. Accomplishments should be celebrated and marked as milestones on the road to even greater things.

2. How you respond in that achievement is also important. Humility is that quality which allows you to see a broader perspective: others too have done great things, you have yet to do all you will, and your current successes are self-evident.

3. Humility allows you to enjoy your accomplishments, but not at the expense of the feelings of those less successful, or less skilled.

4. Balancing the pride of accomplishment with humility in success deepens the respect others have for you, and encourages them to continue to support your success.

PRIDE VS. HUMILITY

Our ego is one of the key drivers encouraging us to improve, be better, accomplish things, and excel. As such, it is a good thing. However, if we feed it too much or become too focused on ourselves, then it becomes pride, and as such begins to get in the way of what we're trying to achieve in our relationships or other areas of our life.

Pride has a way of contaminating relationships and inhibiting strong, healthy discussion and interaction. Humility is the counterpoint to pride, and is both respected and admired. Humility in an individual allows them to be a better listener, to be more focused on others, and to have a greater appreciation for the contribution of others. However, humility also has an Achilles heel. If we are too humble, then we fail to take charge when we need to, we fail to speak up and give our input for the benefit of others, and we fail to make the long-term impact in the lives of others that we could make if we were more willing to "step up and be counted."

Consequently, maintaining a balance between pride and humility, between ego and contribution, is important. Be mindful of this; read the feedback and signals you receive from others, and seek to stay balanced between these extremes.

Organizations need to identify, recognize, and reward heroes and those whose contributions are clearly stellar. However, those assessments need to include not only the actual achievement of objectives, but also the way in which those objectives were achieved. Individuals who can deliver on their accountabilities in a way that is inclusive of others, giving credit where credit is due, and demonstrating the appropriate amount of humility, will go on to continued success, and are more readily followed by others. Balancing the focus on pride of accomplishment, and humility within that accomplishment, is a crucial mark of corporate maturity, and the sign of a strong leader and a talented individual.

Humility bears no resemblance to timidity; rather it demonstrates discipline and maturity, and is respected by others.

Be quietly proud, avoiding self-centered boasting.

GOOD VS. GREAT

Your time and energy are precious. Spend those resources on a balance between good and great results.

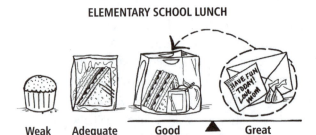

ELEMENTARY SCHOOL LUNCH

Weak   Adequate   Good   ▲   Great

Focus on achieving "great," and reject anything less than good.

1. Be intolerant of results or activities which are either barely adequate, or downright bad.

2. It may look like a "good effort" was made despite unsatisfactory results, and so we're tempted to confuse the effort with the result. Beware of this and don't confuse the two.

3. Concentrate your energy, praise, help, and effort on achieving either good or great results. These are ones which are strong, well-respected, admired, and achieve the intended outcome very effectively.

4. Often times, "great" can take much more in the way of time and effort than the results justify. In this case, "great" is overkill, and unnecessary. Go with "good."

5. Other times, "good" is easy and will do, but "great" would be a much better or more satisfying long-term solution, or impactful approach; then go with great.

GOOD VS. GREAT

Commit yourself to wanting to achieve only those things which are really good and make a significant difference.

Knowing how much energy to put against things that are "good" versus things that are "best" is often challenging. A dad who has decided to spend the afternoon with his son has to choose what would be "good" (for example, taking him to the office with him so at least they're together while the dad works), as opposed to that which is "best" (for example, spending time throwing a Frisbee in the park, going for an ice cream, and then coming home and reading a chapter together in a favorite book). Sometimes it's only possible to do that which is "good," but at least understand that "great" is available, and that this time you have chosen "good" instead of "great," presumably for the right reasons.

However, whenever possible, push for "great." This makes relationships richer, is an investment in the long term, and tends to make experiences far more memorable. Usually, there's a trade-off between "good" and "great" with regards to time, cost, or resources required to move from one to the other. You will have to weigh these up to determine whether it's appropriate to select the "great" option or the "good" option at this time. The important thing is to be aware that there are "great" options, "good" options, and "less than good" options. Know what they are and always select at least the "good," and preferably the "great" whenever possible.

Mediocrity in a competitor is a huge advantage to any organization striving for excellence. Consequently, each organization must themselves avoid mediocrity at all times and in all things. Allocating excessive resources for a relatively minor outcome in order to ensure that it's great may not be the wisest course of action when good in that particular situation will suffice. This allows you to direct the resources to achieve greatness to those areas which are truly significant and provide a meaningful return.

Balance the effort you'll have to make against the results you'll achieve, when trying to decide whether to stop at "good" or go on to "great."

**Always go to "good" and then,
when appropriate, on to "great."**

INFLUENCED VS. INDEPENDENT

Influence should be added nutrition to the giant oak of your life, not stakes and cables supporting an undernourished sapling.

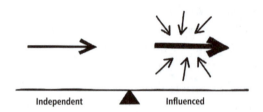

Independent   ▲   Influenced

Value influence, but only after you've fully assessed the source of the influence.

1. Learning to act independently, and then doing so consistently, is an important personal attribute. It's part of what contributes to strong personal character.

2. Exposing yourself to those with greater wisdom, skill, or experience, and allowing them to influence you, can often accelerate your progress or enrich your life.

3. Finding the balance between these two often requires the wisdom of Solomon. Being too independent may cause you to miss a considerable number of opportunities. Being too heavily influenced may cause you to lose the power of personal conviction. However, by constantly assessing, "How well am I balancing these two forces?" you stand a far better chance of getting it right than if you never assessed the issue of balance between them at all.

4. Beware whom you allow into your life as an influencer! Make absolutely certain you know not only what they have to say, but also what they do, what they have done, and the impact they've had on others.

INFLUENCED VS. INDEPENDENT

When we find ourselves being heavily influenced by the way in which somebody manages us, we tend to almost automatically emulate that style, rather than pausing to first consider if in fact it's a style which we really want as our own, or to become skilled at.

We need to balance the desire to grow and be independent, think independently, and learn skills for ourselves, against the opportunity to learn from others, learn from their experience and insight, and to benefit from the influence which they can have on our lives.

Being conscious of this balance between learning through others – allowing them to influence our thoughts, our approaches to life, our values, and even sometimes our beliefs – against acquiring convictions for ourselves as a result of our own thinking and observations, is challenging. We must not reject one approach out of hand simply because the other is immediately available at the moment, or is easy, or is less fraught with problems. We need to embrace both, and help those with whom we associate to embrace both, but also to maintain balance between the two, so that the best of both are present, and neither dominates.

Influence in and of itself is not bad. Bad influence is bad. We need to ensure that those with whom we are associating are enriching our lives; and also give thought to this for those who we are influencing in turn.

Independent thinking is something which is highly valued in that it brings freshness, originality, and personal focus to the task. Learning from others is also highly valued as it allows corporate knowledge to pass on, skills to be transferred, and key character traits to be replicated throughout an organization. There always needs to be balance between the value of individual thought, and being influenced by the attitudes and achievements of others. Without this balance, individuals can become either egocentric (too independent), or repressed (too heavy influenced). Encouraging an appropriate balance between these two is a crucial element of creating an effective workforce over the long term.

A powerful way to personally grow is by developing strong personal independence in conjunction with carefully selected influencers.

Know well by whom you're being influenced.

Demonstrate Character

Leave It Better

Enrich Others

Smile

Contribute

Initiative

Tolerance

LEAVE IT BETTER

Be mindful of opportunities to make a place or a situation better than you found it as a result of your intentional actions.

Pre   Post

Leave things better than you found them.

1. As a matter of habit, when you're finished somewhere, or with something, leave it better than you found it.

2. Having this approach applies to every area of your life: from staying for the weekend at a friend's guest cottage (bring and leave a small tin of candy for the next guest), to using the kitchen (empty and wipe off the toaster), to putting the room in order after a meeting (wipe the whiteboard).

3. It doesn't have to be a big thing; often a little bit extra will go a long way — it'll improve the place you were, show thoughtfulness, and make it easier on the next person.

4. Living this way is applying self discipline to many little situations, which in turn creates a cumulative impact on those in your personal world, and on those influenced by your personal value system.

LEAVE IT BETTER

To leave a place better than you found it is to leave your mark on that place. By virtue of you personally having been there, that particular location has been enriched in some fashion. It could be temporary, such as emptying the waste basket or leaving a thank you card in a friend's guest room, or more permanent, such as creating a more effective way to greet customers.

This mindset moves you to a place of consideration for others. Those that follow you will know that you have been there and appreciate your extra effort. Also, this approach to life is a mark of character that demonstrates thoughtfulness rather than selfishness.

This same principle applies when dealing with other people. In your conversations with others, attempt to leave the people with whom you've come into contact better than you found them. This may perhaps require a word of encouragement, a listening ear, a suggestion, or some advice on where they could go to get information or assistance to further their own aims.

If, after being with you, people leave feeling more encouraged, motivated, or determined, then you have enriched their lives; as a result of that conversation they will leave better than they arrived.

Organizations hold individuals accountable for improvement. If you're managing or leading people, they need to grow stronger under your leadership, improving their skills and competencies. If you're responsible for processes, these need to be improved to show increases in efficiency; if you're responsible for customer service, then relationships with customers need to grow stronger and so benefit the organization. Constant improvement is a recurring theme and each individual needs to make it a personal focus. Anything you touch or are responsible for should be better as a result of you having been responsible for it.

Think about how you can leave something a bit better, and not only about what needs to be done to get it finished.

105%

Enhance your world by your actions.

ENRICH OTHERS

One of the little ways in which you can show you care
for others is by taking the extra time needed to better understand
things from their perspective.

Enrich others by making the time to learn more about their perspective.

1. In the midst of our daily busyness, time is always precious. It's precious to all of us — regardless of age, task, or the priority of the moment.

2. When dealing with others, look for opportunities to give up a little of your own time to better understand the things on the minds of those with whom you come into contact, and then respond in a way that enriches their lives.

3. The major ways to do this are:

   • Listen longer — better listening, engaged listening, interactive listening, takes more time, but shows interest, and demonstrates care — and you learn more

   • Remember better — send a card (any reason is OK); lend a book or magazine of common interest; initiate a phone call

   • Surprise more often — a surprise shows you're thinking of them; when it's linked to something they consider meaningful it has great impact

ENRICH OTHERS

Understand the things of major importance to other people, and be mindful of how you can support them in those things.

This attitude of initially attempting to understand what is important to others, and then determining how best to support them, is an important attribute of character. It allows you to enrich the lives of those with whom you're in contact.

At times, people simply value having a friend, in which case being available to chat or listen is all that's required – but it is required. At other times, significant accomplishments in the lives of people could be remembered.

In the midst of our day-to-day lives we need to pause to consider how best we can take a few moments on a regular basis to contribute to those with whom we have frequent contact and demonstrate our care for them. We also demonstrate our own character when we make those extra efforts for others.

Given the importance of individuals within an organization, everything that can be done to strengthen, improve, or enrich others needs to be done; and as a result, the value of each individual's contribution increases. Each individual, and leaders in particular, carry the responsibility for working to improve the relationships they have with others and, if possible, improving the capabilities of those individuals. This focus can include those for whom we are responsible, those who depend on us downstream of our work, or those upstream on whom we ourselves are dependent. This focus on enriching the lives of others also serves to deepen the culture and power of the organization; it reinforces respect for, and the importance of, each individual.

**Your time is a very precious gift
that you can give.**

SMILE

Be mindful of the power of a smile – for yourself, to lighten the moment; for others, to share that moment.

Smile!

1. When you smile, it's a natural reaction for others to smile in return. This immediately creates a more relaxed and less stressful environment.

2. A smile is a way of indicating that it's OK to perhaps consider another viewpoint; it can let you present a more balanced perspective than is typical with the day-to-day business pressures.

3. Smiling is a way of presenting an approachable, engaging attitude. It is neither threatening nor intimidating. People appreciate it when you're approachable.

4. Genuine friendliness must be behind the smile. Using it to artificially disarm, or to be devious, is dishonest.

SMILE

It seems difficult to believe that something as simple as a smile would have the impact that it does. However, when we smile we indicate that we ourselves are comfortable with the present circumstances, and this puts others at ease as well. We allow them to relax knowing that we are relaxed, a very important quality in relationships that are ongoing, and important as we deal with the day-to-day issues of life.

A smile can be fleeting as you pass in the hall, a way of saying hello in a pleasant way, or can be more extended during a discussion which might otherwise be more heated than you would wish.

Unfortunately, as we focus on the more serious issues of life, smiling does not come easily. As we turn to thinking about the issue, focusing on the problem, or intensely concentrating on a solution, it often takes a conscious effort to smile. But make the effort. It lightens the moment and allows for a more balanced look at whatever is under discussion at the moment.

Clearly there's a time when a smile is inappropriate, when it could look like you are making light of somebody's important issue, not seriously attending to what is going on, or trivializing something of value. Be mindful of this and how your smile could be misinterpreted. Ensure that you do not smile simply for the sake of the smile itself, but rather that you do so when it would be appropriate and genuine. As with all aspects of character, judgement is required as to how much of the character trait should be displayed.

The majority of issues we deal with are not life and death ones, and being relaxed and smiling through them lifts the spirits and increases the ease with which the tasks are accomplished. Even in stressful times, a smile or evidence of good humor is often a welcome break and helps restore perspective. Be committed to making this happen.

Recognize the warmth and well-being created when you smile, and use yours often.

Your smile is a reflection of inner calm.

CONTRIBUTE

Appreciate the importance of having everyone contribute, and make a commitment to always do so yourself.

Contribute to a situation whenever you are able to do so.

1. Be part of those situations in which you are involved by contributing, and so enriching the experience for everyone.

2. Contributions can be:
   - Ideas and suggestions
   - Enthusiasm
   - Energy
   - Resources ("stuff," money, a location)
   - Experience

3. Be willing to give more to situations than you draw from them. A high degree of contribution may not always be required, or appropriate, but being willing to do so is a good way to initially approach each instance.

4. Your personal engagement, and resulting benefit, will increase in direct relation to your personal participation.

CONTRIBUTE

In most situations, we have a choice whether to contribute or not. We will almost always contribute when we're excited about a project, but when the project or activity is more exciting to someone else, then our own motivation to contribute may not be as high. We may mask it by saying, "I'm too tired," or "I have nothing to add," or "I'm not interested in this." However it's presented, the net result is that our contributions to that particular issue are not as great as they could be.

When we fail to contribute others tend to be more easily discouraged, or end up having to "go it alone" when they had counted on your involvement. Make it a matter of choice each time you're involved with others to contribute in a way that is considered meaningful. You may not always be able to contribute something tangible, such as a skill or a resource, but you can certainly contribute the more intangible things like enthusiasm, interest, and engagement. When we contribute, we show that we care, that we are involved, and that the other person's initiatives are important. This is of particular value when we have agreed to be part of that initiative, and they are looking to us to participate wholeheartedly.

Giving less than a 100% contribution to any task in which we are involved is not an option. Each individual carries an obligation to contribute to their fullest, and pay attention to how best to contribute at all times. The organization does not modify its compensation or investment in individuals based on the degree to which they choose to contribute on a daily basis. Rather, it assumes that the contribution will be in full, and consequently the compensation each pay period is in full. Individuals are both morally obligated to give of their best, and as a matter of principle should do so. Others can then rely on that contribution and become maximally effective, with each individual on the team pulling to their fullest, rather than partially coasting on the efforts of others.

Be willing to contribute, and look proactively for appropriate ways to do so.

As much as possible, match your contributions to apparent needs.

INITIATIVE

Make the extra effort to demonstrate initiative, and use it to significantly help those with whom you're involved.

Show initiative when you're involved with others.

1. Your involvement with a group, helping to complete a task, or in discussion with another, is always an opportunity for you to show initiative.

2. This could take the form of volunteering to do something, suggesting another approach you'd be willing to explore, or seeing an opportunity to move something ahead faster, and then doing something about it.

3. By showing initiative you are significantly adding to an outcome, well beyond simply lending your presence.

4. Initiative is highly valued because it helps take the pressure off of others, and makes sure (your) good ideas are not overlooked. Initiative is a way of showing that you're committed to a successful result (a "win"), not just a meaningful activity ("competing").

5. Showing initiative is an action and, as such, requires proactivity on our part. It must therefore go well beyond intention.

INITIATIVE

Demonstrating initiative is one of the principle ways to move you from the category of "really good" to "really terrific."

When we demonstrate initiative we are showing that we understand what is important, what's happening, and why it's being done. Initiative is our way of saying that we are not only willing to be part of the outcome, but we're also willing to make the outcome better. We're willing to do all we can to improve the situation, to think beyond what we've been asked to do, and to add true value as a result of bringing our own skill and thoughtfulness to the issue.

Initiative is very deeply appreciated by those who have the responsibility for achieving something. When they get your initiative as well as your ability it's an extra bonus.

Initiative is one of the most highly valued qualities within an organization because it gives that organization benefits which they did not otherwise realize were available. Individuals who show initiative identify something, which if done, will improve a situation or outcome, and then proactively contribute it. In doing so, they have clearly demonstrated their commitment and involvement. Initiative should be highly regarded and acknowledged. Demonstrating initiative should be a personal priority we set for ourselves.

By showing initiative, you improve both the end product and your relationships with those involved.

**Your initiative comes from your own
commitment to overall success.**

TOLERANCE

Tolerance for the ideas, thoughts, and reasonable actions of others demonstrates strong self-confidence, and is always greatly appreciated.

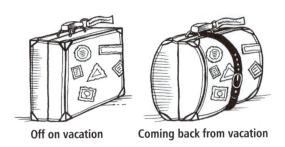

Off on vacation   Coming back from vacation

Demonstrate tolerance of others, rather than rigidity.

1. As that suitcase you packed for the vacation left home "full" but came back "really full" – it showed tolerance – so must we.

2. The suitcase had a shape and operated well as such. But it also had the capability to stretch, to expand. It was built to be tolerant of more, to handle the unexpected, or even the planned-for extras.

3. For us to demonstrate tolerance we need to anticipate that more may be required of us, that we will have to give extra effort, and be willing to stretch. And in so doing we must allow others some grace; instead of responding rigidly towards them, we need to show tolerance, and allow for the fact that they do not exactly "fit our mold."

4. Being tolerant allows us to see the best in others, not just what we want or expect.

TOLERANCE

We each are who we are as a result of the experiences we have had in life, the things that we have learned and seen, been taught, or lived through. Each of these has built convictions within us as to the appropriate course of action in a given situation. It is then often challenging to cope with others who approach a situation differently than we would.

Each of these instances is an opportunity for tolerance. We need to understand that their experiences, and understandings of life, have led them to adopt a different approach. It may differ from our approach entirely or only slightly; nonetheless, it is the approach which they feel to be most appropriate. Without condemning or judging, we need to understand and be tolerant.

Once we have recognized the need for tolerance, we then need to decide whether or not we approve of their approach. Tolerance does not mean approval, rather it means understanding or acceptance. If we do not approve of the approach, then clearly it is something we will not support. But tolerance allows us to see that if it is only a different approach, and not an issue of it being blatantly wrong, then we can be more easily supportive. Learn to distinguish between the things you disapprove of and the areas where you must learn to master tolerance.

Individual uniqueness is something to be valued. Uniqueness brings differences in perspectives, different suggestions, and alternate approaches. These differences can be used to enhance an outcome or accelerate a result; therefore, an organization needs to foster tolerance. This tolerance should not be for behavior or attitudes which are outside of the law or culturally acceptable boundaries, but within those boundaries it is something which needs to be encouraged as it allows individuals to contribute to the full, promotes communication, and increases initiative.

Strive to overcome personal reservations that keep you from being flexible and tolerant.

A demonstration of tolerance is usually reflected by the comment, "Thanks for your understanding."

Build Trust

Relationship

Honesty

Frequency

Integrity

Selfless

Share

RELATIONSHIP

As we seek to develop or deepen relationships, we need to ensure we put focus on building and maintaining trust.

The house of relationship must be built on the foundation of rock solid trust.

1. "Trust" means that you can be relied on. If I know I can rely on you, then we have a basis for an ongoing and meaningful relationship.

2. Some relationships may be casual (for example, with the butcher who says this ground meat has no fat) or intense (for example, with our parents who say they'll help us start up our own company). The greater the trust, the deeper the relationship.

3. Relationships are seen primarily in what we do, and what we say. Consequently, as we build or deepen relationships, we need to be sure that we are doing so on the basis of trust. Two questions can help with this:

   • Will this person be able to completely rely on what I'm saying?

   • Is what I'm doing (or about to do) going to increase (or decrease) this person's trust in me?

RELATIONSHIP

When trust is present in a relationship, then there are many opportunities for that relationship to grow stronger. Individuals are more willing to share their deeper thoughts, how they think, and why they think the way they do. Individuals are more willing to take risks and give you ideas, or thoughts that are still not fully formed, when they know they can trust you to respect the fact that they are still "just thoughts."

As we seek to improve the relationships we have with others we need to demonstrate to them that we can keep confidences, will deliver on our promises, and can be counted on to look after things left in our care. These are manifestations of trust, and as we show ourselves trustworthy in these areas, then others are more willing to entrust themselves, their ideas, and their "thinking" to us.

Once trust is firmly established between individuals, then the relationship can focus on things of much more significant worth than when trust is absent. Troublesome topics, worrying concerns, and exciting futures can all be discussed with greater openness and confidence. As a result, the understanding that exists can go far deeper between the individuals concerned, and as it goes deeper so the relationship itself grows stronger.

For trust to truly be strengthened in a relationship both parties have to be continually willing to trust the other, and with each opportunity give more of themselves to the relationship, each time assessing whether their trust has been maintained. When it has, confidence builds and more things can be shared. Trust is built, not earned; this takes time. Take every opportunity to display or demonstrate trust, and use wisely that which is entrusted to you.

Trust is at the core of ongoing relationships.

HONESTY

As we are able to handle – and want – the full truth, so do those with whom we interact. Doing so builds trust.

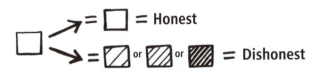

Trust is built on honesty, which means the full truth, not shades of grey.

1. Honesty means presenting the entire truth as you know it.

2. Half-truths ("That's all they asked about"), part of the truth, truth with buried bias – all of these are not considered "being honest." In fact, if they leave the impression of honesty when not being fully so, then they're actually dishonest.

3. Often, being honest requires first that you get a clear understanding of the other person's requirements (for information, detail, or insight). This then allows you to know how much, and what, to include.

4. Honesty does not mean callousness or insensitivity. In difficult situations, when honesty is called for, tact and consideration can, and should, be used.

HONESTY

Honesty means that we have truly communicated not only the facts but also the essence of those facts. Honesty means that we have in no way dissembled, or sought to present only an aspect of the truth, knowing that it will be seen as if it were the whole truth, when we know in our heart that in fact the whole truth was not effectively communicated.

One of the traps that we can fall into is captured by expressions such as "Well, they didn't ask about that," or, "Well, that would have just hurt them." When you set out to be honest, the true test is whether or not the other person is left knowing what you know, and has the same amount of fact and information that you do on which to base their conclusions. If you hold things back, or convince yourself that maybe it's not appropriate to share everything at this point, then you have perhaps not been entirely honest.

This is not to say that it is necessary to say everything to everybody we know. You must choose what to share and when, and what to withhold. The issue is that if you do choose to withhold information, then it is important that the other person realizes that you have made this choice for some reason. It is not good if you give the impression that you have been totally honest, giving everything you have available, when you have not. On the other hand, it is quite acceptable to be completely truthful in what you say, but also to make it clear that for some reason, which you feel to be the wisest course of action, you have chosen not to share everything.

There can be no trust without honesty. Speaking the truth, and doing so with the appropriate tact, is essential to ensure long-term sustained trust, productive relationships, and worthwhile outcomes.

Building trust requires those involved to bring intentional, considered honesty to the relationship.

Honesty is a key ingredient to building trust.

FREQUENCY

Understand the importance of meeting together, and make it a priority, if you are committed to building trust with one another.

Connecting frequently as time passes allows trust to grow.

1. Trust, like relationships, needs contact to flourish.

2. In order to build trust, opportunities to be together need to be seized or, if there aren't enough already, made.

3. When people are together, they get to know one another better; they remain in touch with the issues of the moment, and can participate in one another's day-to-day concerns, joys, decisions, or challenges. This builds trust.

4. Then, when they're apart, there is more common understanding and experience to fall back on when it's necessary to do so.

5. Trust is one of the results that comes from seeing a consistency in behavior and speech; and consistency requires frequency.

FREQUENCY

As much as possible, make frequent contact with those with whom you are attempting to build trust and establish a relationship. Frequent contact enables you to stay in tune with one another, and makes it easier to close any gap which needs to be closed when you reconnect.

Building trust is easy when there's not a lot of ground to cover since last you met. When it's been a long time between connections, then much will have occurred which can be shared but isn't because of the time it would take, or simply not remembering all that has happened.

Connecting frequently keeps the channels of communication open, eliminates the opportunity for misunderstanding, and allows collaboration to flourish. Trust then remains strong, and distance, or absence, does not serve as an impediment to maintaining a strong relationship between the two of you.

During the hectic pace of day-to-day operations we often "touch base" with individuals, but we need to go further and "connect." This is making the effort to take a few extra minutes wherever possible to make a personal, deeper connection than simply a passing hello. Clearly this is not required at all times, but it needs to be demonstrated that we recognize those with whom we deal are people with lives apart from work. When appropriate, move the conversation to include reference to these other, often deeper, priorities of the individuals with whom you deal. This demonstrates a frank concern for them as people, and is a component in building trust.

Make it a priority to meet frequently with those with whom you feel it's important to build, and maintain, trust.

**Meeting frequently is an
important way to build trust.**

INTEGRITY

Work hard to ensure your integrity is solid as perceived by others, not just in your own opinion. Get feedback to ensure you know the perspective of others.

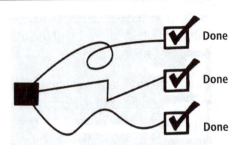

Integrity is doing what you say you will do, and essential to building trust.

1. Integrity is that quality which makes us dependable. Reliable. "A person of their word."

2. Integrity needs to be shown in two areas:

   • When you commit to something measurable, (e.g., by a certain time or date, or with a specific action: "I'll do...," "I'll take...," "I'll give...")

   • When you state an intention, (e.g., "You can count on me in this" or "Trust me")

3. In both areas, the person to whom you're talking will have a mental picture of what you mean. Be sure you take a moment to see that they see this picture in the same way as you do, because they'll be assessing your integrity against their picture (not yours).

4. In the same way that you can't lean safely on a rickety and rotten old fence, you can't build trust with someone who lacks integrity. Without integrity there can be no trust.

INTEGRITY

If we wish to build trust, then "our word must be our bond." This is a very important element of trust in that very often all people have to go on is what we say, and then whether we do what we say we'll do. Maintaining this link between doing and saying, so that we are clearly perceived to be reliable, is building integrity. With integrity comes trust. It is much easier to trust someone who can be relied on to do what they say than someone who is erratic, or someone who perhaps has good intentions, but is essentially unreliable.

When focusing on integrity, we need to make sure that what we say we'll do, and what others understand we mean by what we say, are the same thing.

Integrity within an organization is crucial to an organization's efficiency. Individuals that cannot be relied upon to do what they say they will do require large amounts of wasted management time documenting, following up, reinforcing, notating, and reminding. Integrity must be the key mandate at all times and a key priority for all individuals. Integrity includes delivering on clearly articulated promises, and also on implied promises. Clearly for trust to exist in an organization there must be a high degree of integrity among all those concerned, and confidence there won't be compromise to commitments or promised results.

As you work to build trust with others, ensure your personal integrity is high, and that you look for the same in others.

Trust relies on the integrity of both people.

SELFLESS

Be mindful, and focused, on the issues of others with whom you are building trust, rather than primarily on yourself.

Periodically move the focus off of "self" and on to others.

1. When your focus is on others – those with whom you're building trust – then it quickly becomes evident that your interest lies with their interests, and this builds trust.

2. By showing that it's not only your ideas, your thoughts, your wishes, and your perceptions that are important, but theirs as well, you create a climate where trust can flow easily.

3. You'll consider giving your trust to those who demonstrate that your interests, priorities, and thoughts are important to them. As they are clearly willing to move their focus from themselves to you, then you're much more open to trusting them. And if this focus (on your interests) persists, then your confidence in them, and so your trust, builds.

4. But the focus on others must be sincere, well-intentioned, and real; otherwise, it's perceived as deceitful, and ultimately a major roadblock to building trust.

SELFLESS

When we are self-centered what we are essentially saying is that we are the center of the universe and others must revolve around us. It is hard to trust someone who has that perspective, because it's difficult to know whether or not they can be relied on to see other perspectives, and to act with the interest of others in mind as well as their own.

Consequently as we seek to build trust with others, we need to avoid becoming preoccupied with our own selves. Essentially, this means that we need to be mindful of others, their needs, their priorities, and their issues, and be able to respond to them. This is not to say that we should have little focus or attention on ourselves, but rather to say that all the attention and focus should not be on ourselves. We are inclined to trust those who we believe have our interests at heart. Doing so requires a degree of selflessness on their part.

Individuals within an organization are focused on achieving their own accountabilities. This is what they are compensated for and what they have committed to deliver. Each individual is in the same situation; so it is important that as you move forward to deliver on your accountabilities, you do not forget that others are moving forward with an equal degree of intensity on their own accountabilities. Where possible, demonstrate an appreciation for the things that are key to them; by doing so you increase the trust between you. When others know that you are willing, at times, to put their needs ahead of your own, then they come to appreciate that you can be relied upon when they call upon you in time of need. This degree of confidence that has grown between individuals increases the trust between them, and improves the organization's efficiency and effectiveness.

Learn to see the priorities of others, and as appropriate, consider placing them ahead of your own as you seek to strengthen the trust between you and them.

Selflessness enables trust to grow.

SHARE

Be alert for opportunities to share both intangible things (compassion, ideas) and tangible things (resources, time) when building or demonstrating trust.

Trust means a willingness to share.

1. If there is a sharing of ideas, energy, time, or resources, then there is the building of trust.

2. By sharing, I'm indicating that I trust you'll benefit from what I'm sharing. If on your part you use or apply what's shared as intended, my trust is validated and we've grown closer.

3. Often one person can't fully appreciate the needs and, therefore, the requests of another. If, in spite of that, sharing occurs to meet those needs, then trust is demonstrated:

   • By the person asking ("I trust you'll understand")

   • By the person sharing ("I trust you, and therefore am willing to share")

4. Sharing builds trust, demonstrates trust, deepens trust, and confirms trust.

SHARE

Sharing is a demonstrated act whereby you take something which is yours and you allow others to use it or have it. In doing so you are implicitly indicating that you trust that person will value what you have shared, and appreciate it. You have also used your resources in some way to enrich them. Every time this happens, trust increases.

As with all of these aspects of trust, actions must be reciprocal if the trust is to grow and be sustained. If you are constantly sharing and others are only taking, then quickly you will feel taken advantage of, and trust will not grow, but be destroyed. You will begin to feel that you cannot "trust" the other to truly value what you are sharing as you intended. Sharing between individuals is a tangible way to put the desire for increased trust into action, and is an important ingredient in building trust with others.

One aspect of selflessness is the sharing of resources, time, or energy. It is rare that we need absolutely everything that we have in order to fulfill our own accountabilities. Hoarding those resources for the eventuality of perhaps needing them is not always the wisest course of action. If your contingencies are covered, then sharing will accelerate the progress of others; if done throughout the whole organization, the progress of the group as a whole accelerates. This is especially evident within a team environment, where the needs of the team must supersede the needs of the individual; consequently, all resources available need to be the property of the team and shared among the team members. When this is done effectively, then significant trust develops within the team, allowing it to accelerate its performance well beyond that of a team whose attitude is "each one must look out for themself."

Recognize the importance of sharing in building trust. But also recognize the responsibility not to betray the trust that has been demonstrated by sharing.

Sharing contributes to building trust.

Get Things Done

Desired Outcome

Available Resources

To Do List

Prioritize

Contingencies

Time to Plan

DESIRED OUTCOME

*Plan what you'll do based on clearly identifying
what it is to look like after you've done it.*

Before starting, have a clear mental picture of
the desired outcome.

1. When you plant a garden in the spring you must first know which flowers, of which colors, and how many of each, you want, and in which locations; that is, how you want it to look when they all start to bloom.

2. So with getting the most done in the time available – the better you know what you want the outcome to look like, the easier it is to direct all your energies to that outcome, and not get sidetracked.

3. For example, assume you've decided to improve customer service for an important client. How often should you meet? What will they want to see? With whom would they appreciate meeting? What assumptions are currently being made? Are these correct? The better you can answer these questions to picture the desired outcome, the easier it will be to plan, and then work towards the task.

4. Once underway concentrate on achieving your mental picture, and nothing else, at this time. Stick to bringing your picture to life, then plan your next "picture."

DESIRED OUTCOME

When you create a mental picture of the finished outcome, try to make that picture as complete as possible. The more accurately you can describe how it will look when it's done, the more accurately you can plan it out.

Sometimes we think we know what it will look like, but we really have only a fuzzy picture in mind, a sort of "general direction." Often a good way to make sure that the mental picture is clear is to describe it to someone else. Let them ask questions where they're unclear about what you mean, and then in the process of answering them you will get greater clarity yourself.

For example, if you decide to organize a surprise birthday party for your spouse, then besides deciding who to invite, what to do, and what food to have, picture the party completely. Will everyone be asked to bring a gift that follows a theme? Where will the food be placed around the house? What will the kids' roles be? What will be the decorations? Where will they be placed? What will be the first thing noticed as you walk in the front door? The better you are able to picture the party in your mind in its entirety, the better you will be able to plan a great event.

Doing this thinking in advance takes a few extra minutes, but it's well worth it. It often keeps you from backtracking or missing anything important, and allows you to use your time most efficiently once you get going.

Organizations working towards achievement of an outcome need a clear statement of that outcome. This clarity is best ensured when it is fully detailed in writing, storyboards, etc., as then there can be no uncertainty about what is meant, and in its crafting all possible interpretations are discussed and clarified. Whether working in a team environment or on an individual project or assignment, a clear picture of what is to be accomplished needs to be developed. A test for clarity is to then show the result to others to see if they draw the same conclusions of the foreseen outcome that was intended when it was originally created by the creators.

Create a plan based on first determining exactly what you want to accomplish.

Picture it done, and then bring it to life.

AVAILABLE RESOURCES

*Identify what you have to work with in terms of
time and resources before you begin your plan. You may need
to then modify your desired outcome as a result.*

**Know in advance what resources are available,
and set your goal accordingly.**

1. Before beginning, know what you have available to work with in terms of:

   • Time

   • People to help

   • Energy

   • Money

   • Space

2. Then create your plan based on these resources. It's important to realize we may not be able to do all we want because we don't have enough of something available.

3. Be realistic in terms of what you can accomplish this time around. Doing this keeps you from eating into the resources you need for the next thing – which can then just become a vicious circle of never getting anything done properly.

AVAILABLE RESOURCES

Before beginning a task or project, it's crucial to know what you have available to work with. To get started on a project, then discover that you don't have enough to finish it, can be frustrating. Equally frustrating is finishing the project and realizing you didn't need all the resources you'd accumulated.

Usually the most crucial resource, and the one hardest to gauge, is time. The other ones tend to be easier to plot out and predict. Somehow most things tend to take much longer than we anticipate. In order to adjust for this, make sure you allow a lot of extra time, so that you don't run out of time or find yourself rushing at the end.

Knowing clearly what resources you have, and will need, before you begin is a great way to ensure you complete each task as and when intended. This identification and confirmation of available resources allows you to move ahead with the confidence that you'll have what's required to deliver on your promised outcome.

Know what you have to work with and set your expectations, and therefore your plan, accordingly.

Tailor-make your plan to match your resources.

TO DO LIST

Begin by listing all that needs to be done – this lets you allocate your time, energy, and resources so as to produce the best results.

Make a To Do List.

1. By making a To Do List, you capture everything that needs doing; then, you can focus on accomplishment, rather than trying to remember things.

2. Your To Do Lists can fall into the following categories:

   • Do today

   • Do this week

   • Do this month

   • Do some day

3. Then each week you can check the lists to see what should get moved up (from "this week" to "today," or "some day" to "this month," etc.).

4. To Do Lists can be:

   • For all the separate things you want to do, broken down as listed above (i.e., "today," "this week," etc.); they can be big things or smaller tasks

   • For the smaller tasks within one big thing (e.g., "hire staff" is a big thing; "write a job description," "post job," are the smaller tasks)

TO DO LIST

To make the most of your time and the resources that you have, a To Do List lets you focus your attention on the key things that you want to accomplish. Without it, we tend to drift from task to task, not always sure what is either the right thing at the moment, or how much time to give it. When you're working from To Do Lists, then you have a target for what you want to complete by the end of each day, which then lets you better decide how much time to give to each task. It also allows you to know what it is you will be doing today, and what it is you won't be doing.

To Do Lists should really be a tool to help you, not a slave driver to force you into action. They can be all-inclusive as indicated above, or they can be short and abbreviated, made up of only the major tasks to be accomplished throughout the day, in which case you know you'll intersperse those tasks with other things that must be done, so they don't need to be on the list.

The main thing to remember is to add things to your To Do List as they come up during the day and which, if you don't put them on the list, probably won't get done. They may not get done today, or even need to be done today, but they will have to be done at some point, so need to be on the list. In order to ensure that you achieve everything that needs to be done, your To Do List grows as the number of tasks increases. Items are then crossed off as they are completed.

Working off the To Do List ensures that your obligations can be reviewed frequently to ensure proper priorities are assigned, foreseen resources are allocated (including time required), and important items will not be neglected.

Use To Do Lists to keep organized, stay focused, and be efficient. They are an amazing planning tool.

**Make up To Do Lists as your
first task each day.**

PRIORITIZE

Make sure you always put the most important things at the top of your To Do List, and then work top down.

Always do the most important things first.

1. You need to know for any To Do List (today, this week, etc.) what's the most important.

2. Then...do that first.

3. If it's short, and you think, "Oh, it's short and simple, I'll do it later"...don't. Do it first!

4. If it's long and more complicated, break it into smaller To Do's, put them in priority, and get started on number 1.

5. If you do the most important things first, then:

   • They get the necessary time, energy, resources, etc.

   • They get done!

   • They're off your mind

   • They can't get "unavoidably incomplete" because something else "took longer" or "was harder" than foreseen

6. If it's the most important thing to have done – do it first. Number 2 then becomes number 1, and so forth. In the end, if something doesn't get done, it will be the least important, not the most!

PRIORITIZE

Somehow it seems that very often the thing which is really most important, and which absolutely must get done today, is not necessarily the most interesting and engaging thing. Perhaps it takes longer to do, or we've been procrastinating, or it's something which we'd really rather not do, despite it's importance.

In this case, it's absolutely crucial that we do it first. If we dream up some excuse for not doing it first, then the chances are that by the end of the day it won't be done, but we will have created a lot of great reasons why it wasn't!

The biggest challenge is that either the thing can't be done right now or it's quite large, and you have to get a few smaller things done first. If either of these is the case, then you clearly can't do it first, but you will need to set a time when you will start it. This may even mean stopping something else that you are in the middle of in order to start it, but if that's the situation, you'll have to do so and come back and finish the other task afterwards. This way you're sure to always end the day with the most important things done.

If you adopt this approach, the things that need to be done each day grow less and less important (because you're getting the most important things knocked off one by one), so that in due time you'll have more flexibility as to how you spend your time.

The priorities of the organization should be the priorities on which we operate. In order to ensure this happens, we need to rank items on our To Do List in that order of priority. This priority is established in conjunction with your leader, and previously agreed objectives. In this way your time and energy is aligned with the expectations of the organization and its leadership.

Know what's most important, and make it your priority to do that first.

Focus first on your first priority.

CONTINGENCIES

Commit to seeing a task through to completion, by being prepared with answers to possible "what if" questions.

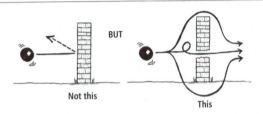

Be prepared for roadblocks by having contingency plans.

1. Don't let roadblocks, hurdles, or "brick walls" stop you from completing your plan. Before you start, create a contingency (or "what if") plan. Some examples:

What if:	Then:
• Out of time	• Use the time originally intended for a lower priority task
	• Add it to tomorrow's list
	• Try a different (shorter) method
• Out of resources	• Break it into smaller pieces
	• Get help
	• Do only the most urgent now
• Job is bigger than I thought	• Try a creative, unintended approach
	• Have planned-for "on call" resources
	• Try to put two desired outcomes together and share resources between both

2. What contingencies you come up with aren't as important as having them. Know what you'll do if a roadblock occurs.

CONTINGENCIES

It's unrealistic to assume that all our plans are going to flow smoothly without hiccups or the unforeseen happening. Yet somehow, we never seem to allow enough time to deal with these unforeseen events, nor do we actually plan for them. That's probably because we're optimistic and are always hoping for the best. This is a good thing, but one that can sometimes cause frustration when things don't go as hoped.

A good way to deal with this is to look at your To Do List and pick out the two or three major things where you anticipate something could go wrong, or take longer than you planned. Once you've identified these then create some contingency plans, asking yourself how you would deal with any likely hiccups. You might decide to set aside some extra time in the event that you run into a problem, or you may in fact be able to identify a few specific fallback actions if you've been there before and know what is likely to occur.

The key is to plan the approach you'll take if you hit a hurdle, and set aside the time to deal with it. In this way, your daily plan is more accurate, has made provision for the unforeseen, and can progress smoothly. If, at the end of the day no problems materialize, then that's a bonus and you have extra time. But it's better to end the day with extra time and everything done than feeling pressured because you didn't get everything done, and are now "behind the eight ball!"

Each day, always set aside a little emergency time with nothing scheduled. Then, if you run into a snag, you can use some of that emergency time to deal with it without throwing your whole day's schedule off track. If you're not sure how much to set aside, then simply decide on something that looks reasonable, and refine it each day until you become more accurate at deciding how much emergency time you require.

Be prepared with answers for any "what if" issues which may surface, so the task doesn't have to be abandoned.

Often hurdles serve to generate very creative and effective alternatives.

TIME TO PLAN

Commit to making time to plan before acting.
The planning step is the first step of any action.

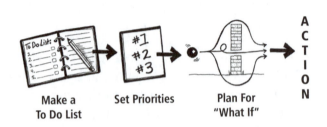

Make a   Set Priorities   Plan For
To Do List   "What If"

Take the time, up-front, to plan before taking action.

1. It's human nature to want to "get started," to just "jump right into it," and this initiative is a great thing; however, the first thing to jump into is the planning, not the doing.

2. Work through the planning steps:

   • List To Do's

   • Put them in priority sequence

   • Consider "what ifs"

3. This doesn't have to take long (and it becomes faster with practice), but it must be done first.

4. This up-front planning ensures you allocate your time, energy, and resources where they're most needed today, and it pays back many times over in efficiency.

5. Begin each initiative, each task, and each day with a few minutes set aside to plan.

TIME TO PLAN

Sometimes, when we set aside time to plan, we find ourselves wondering whether it would be better to be actually "doing" rather than "planning." There's rarely a better use of our time than the time that we spend planning. The only exception to this is when we use "I need to plan" as an excuse for not actually getting down to work!

The power of planning is so strong because it allows us to think through what we're going to do, what needs to be done, how we're going to do it, and what might go wrong before we ever actually do anything. Planning is a bit like doing things mentally before we do them in practice. As a result, we're better able to make changes or adjustments, because we're only changing what we're thinking about; we're not actually spending time driving back from somewhere, or rushing to finish something, or frantically calling for help at the last minute. If, during the planning stages, we do it all in our mind first, then we're better able to lay out a plan that is realistic and practical.

Sometimes it's hard to discipline ourselves to actually sit and do the planning that's required, but it quickly pays the time back as the day unfolds and your schedule is now more realistic; the most important things have been identified up-front, and some thinking about contingencies has already been done. The more we value the time to plan, the more effectively we'll be able to accomplish all that we want to do.

Once you've put all that time into planning, make sure you then stick to your plan!

Plan first, then rush off to action.

Planning is the initial thrust that ensures your success.

Make Suggestions

Clearly Presented

Adapt to the Listener

Thought-out

Open-minded

Improve On It

Practical

CLEARLY PRESENTED

Clearly understood suggestions are easier to act on and evaluate.
Take the extra time to be really clear.

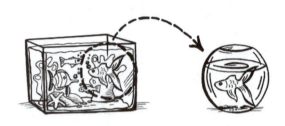

Make one suggestion at a time, each clearly presented.

1. We often have several suggestions to make on a given topic or issue; however, it's most effective if you present just one at a time, and present each very clearly.

2. "Clearly" means that the other person knows what your idea is, and why you've suggested it. This means you'll have to put a little extra effort into what you say. Bear in mind three things:

   • Work out exactly what your suggestion is, telling it to yourself before you start to speak; this will make sure it's clear to you!

   • Imagine them hearing your words, but hearing them with their own ideas, biases, and personality

   • Adapt what you were going to say so it makes sense to them, from their perspective, as well as from your own

3. This extra effort to be really clear will usually mean your suggestion will get more attention and consideration.

CLEARLY PRESENTED

When we're very enthusiastic, and excited to contribute, there are times when we don't seem to make much sense to anyone but ourselves! We need to remember that the people we're talking to haven't yet had a chance to follow the thought process we took to arrive at our ideas, so if we don't present them clearly, the others will be lost. If we remember this, then we'll take a few extra minutes to make sure we present things in a way that makes sense to them.

For example, if a group of friends are sitting around discussing what they should do, and you throw out the following idea: "Let's start a dinner club; it would be fun, and we'd get to know other countries!" your idea may not get the attention or value it deserves because it's not well understood. An alternative would be to say: "Instead of getting together and always wondering what to do, let's decide on one fun and interesting thing that we could do together for a while. For example, if we get together every week, we could agree to selecting one country that would be our theme country for that night."

"Then we would each bring a component of a meal that is typical of that country. We'd agree up-front who would bring the appetizers, the main course, the dessert, the drinks, etc., and each of those roles could rotate each week. In this way we would learn something about different countries, we'd get to try different foods, and we wouldn't always be wondering what to do together." Your suggestion maybe took a little longer to give (but not much), but more importantly, it gave people a sense of what your idea was and why. This then makes it easier to value it, and either act on it, or use it as a springboard for something else.

An organization places great value on the suggestions which individuals bring. You have the responsibility to ensure your suggestions are clearly presented in order to maximize the time of those involved in reviewing the suggestion, as well as to ensure that good ideas are not lost because they were poorly presented. It is your responsibility to ensure your suggestions are clearly presented, not just to come up with them.

Mentally rehearse your words, as heard from the listener's perspective, before you speak.

When it's really clear, it's more easily understood.

ADAPT TO THE LISTENER

Value your suggestion enough to take the extra time to package it in a way that will ensure it will be received as intended.

Be very mindful of your audience and adapt your words accordingly.

1. Almost always our approach to issues, even how we speak and what we mean by our words, is different (sometimes a lot, sometimes a little) from the approach of the person we're talking with.

2. We need to adapt what we say so it is effectively received by the one to whom we're talking.

3. Our great suggestion could be a square peg from a square hole (us) going to a round hole (them) — we have to change the peg from square to round, so it fits.

4. Changing the shape of the peg is not changing the suggestion. Rather it's using words, or examples, that allows us to talk in terms that are familiar to them.

5. It's very important to adapt how you present the suggestion. Otherwise, in your enthusiasm for the idea, you try to jam its original package and how it naturally comes from you (square peg) into a round hole, and both the suggestion and the intent are lost. Adapt your words first.

ADAPT TO THE LISTENER

How well you understand your audience, and reflect that understanding in your suggestion, often determines how well your suggestion is received. If you suggest to your 10-year-old daughter that she "redecorate her room," the response you get could likely be very different from the response you would get from your spouse.

With your daughter, "redecorate" in her mind probably means getting rid of all the things which she likes in her room – the teddy bears, pictures on the wall, and favorite books – and so her immediate response is probably "No." What you had intended was to repaint the walls and molding to update it. You had perhaps envisioned changing the curtains and bedspread to better match her current interests, and putting up a series of shelves so she would have more room for her teddy bears and knickknacks. Once this was understood, her response would most likely be "Great! Let's do it!"

In order to avoid the trauma and the possible frustration of having to move from "No!" to "Great!" you need to be sure that your suggestion is adapted to the other's perspective. In this case, you might have said something like, "Let's take a look at how we can change your room so that you like it even more." In this way, you've made a similar suggestion, but dramatically changed the way you presented it to adapt it to the listener. This does not change the intent, but it certainly does change the way in which your suggestion is received.

We need to make the effort required to craft our suggestion in terms which others will understand.

A powerful suggestion is only powerful if it's understood when it's received.

Think about both message and delivery.

THOUGHT-OUT

*Understand what your suggestion will mean in practice,
and be able to explain it.*

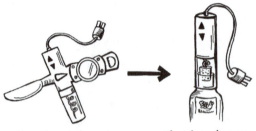

**Electric corkscrew, jar
opener, butter spreader, and
beer bottle opener**

Electric corkscrew

Think through the consequences of your suggestions.

1. People will appreciate your suggestions more if you've thought them through before you make them.

2. In this way, if an idea has some wacky components and some great components, it doesn't all get lost if only the wacky part is noticed.

3. You don't have to necessarily edit out the wacky parts (although you may want to), but by thinking it through before you present it, you can add some commentary. For example: "Here's the idea. It has some wacky parts, but I think they may help us come up with great ideas; what do you think?"

4. When thinking your suggestion through to assess its merit, ask yourself these two questions. The answers will help you better understand your own suggestion, and so improve how you present it.

    • What would be the consequences of trying to implement it?

    • If implemented, what would be the impact?

THOUGHT-OUT

We show respect for others when the ideas we present have been thought through. By presenting the first thing that comes into our mind we are requiring our listeners to both figure out the implication of the suggestion and to assess it as well.

When you've first taken a few moments to think through the consequences then you may be able to edit out some of the less practical pieces, so that when you present the suggestion it has more value, and as such the listeners can take it and begin working with it right away. This requires that you think through what your idea is before you present it, and mentally do a quick check to determine how feasible it is, as well as what some of the consequences would be if in fact it were to be implemented as you originally intended.

After thinking it through like this you may be able to trim away some of the elements which, on reflection, are not at all practical, and possibly even add a couple of pieces to make it more effective.

Knowing how to edit your suggestion is done simply by thinking through the implications and consequences of your suggestion if it were to be implemented in its entirety, and then assessing how practical that is. From that assessment, you can begin to modify your suggestion before you present it.

Within a corporation, when ideas are put forward or requested, there's an expectation that they'll be well thought through, the consequences of the idea, if implemented, will have been considered and the implications also considered. Bear this in mind when you present your ideas so they can have maximum impact and can be moved to implementation as quickly as possible.

Present well thought-out suggestions. Others will really appreciate it.

Understand the implications of your suggestions.

OPEN-MINDED

Each idea you present is valuable – whether it's taken unchanged and applied as is, or used as a springboard for something even more effective. Be open to both.

Be open-minded to possible unforeseen directions to which your suggestions may lead.

1. As you wander through a forest, your woodland path may have many forks. In a similar way, an original suggestion may ultimately lead through different forks to an unforeseen place.

2. Usually this is a result of others hearing your suggestion, and upon considering it, thinking of ways to adopt it, apply it, or improve upon it.

3. If, as a result of this approach, the end destination is even better than the original one – something that often happens when this kind of open discussion occurs – then that's good!

4. You need to remain flexible and open-minded to your idea being changed in this way, rather than trying to protect and defend it. Sometimes the original idea was best and you'll want to come back to it; sometimes what is generated is better. Be part of the process, and value your original contribution for what it led to.

OPEN-MINDED

When discussing ideas with others, it's often easy to have a particular favorite – your own! Very often the things we think of seem to us to be the best ideas. Partly this is because we thought them up ourselves in the first place, but more often it is because we understand our idea and the implications of it better than we understand others' ideas and their implications. Even though we initially intend to favor our own ideas, it's important that we develop the ability to concentrate on what would be best overall – not only for ourselves but for everyone – and to recognize how our suggestions can be modified or shaped to create an even better idea.

When working within a group, and trying to come up with the best possible approach based on the input and suggestions of others, you need to think of this a bit like trying to create a beautiful piece of pottery. The potter puts the clay on the wheel and begins spinning it, and under his hands a beautiful pot slowly emerges. Similarly, ideas initially presented are like the clay that everyone in the group can begin to work on. As each person works with it, by giving more ideas, suggestions, modifications, or input, then slowly under the collective hands of all concerned, those early ideas are shaped into something that ultimately becomes a really top notch suggestion. The shaping process, and the final solution, belong to no one individual, but rather are the collective result of everyone working on it together. Consequently, you need to be willing to let this happen and not take too great an ownership of your own personal ideas, but rather be part of the overall collective result of the group's work.

Ideas are "your" ideas at the time of conception, but once put forward they become the property of the team or the organization. Ultimately, the organization will benefit much more if you choose to support improvements to your original suggestion.

Be open to your idea leading to other, perhaps better, ones and participate throughout the discussion.

Ideas can grow, but only
after the first one is presented!

IMPROVE ON IT

Explore the options that can be created from your original suggestion to get the best and most satisfying result.

Once a great suggestion has been made, try to improve on it.

1. A suggestion that is well received can be implemented as is, or a few extra minutes can be taken to see if it can be enhanced. This is not only fun to do, but can sometimes yield a large payoff.

2. Some questions to ask when trying to improve on good suggestions:

   • If we had only half as much money, time, space, or effort, how could we still make it happen?

   • If a famous painter, poet, musician, or movie director were doing this, how would they do it?

   • If we had to do this in space, underwater, in the Amazon jungle, or in the desert, how would we do it?

   • If this was all we had to do, how would we do it?

3. The answers you get from these questions can be thought starters, and a basis for more and more ideas as you think about each new thought. Ultimately you'll have to stop and reign in all the ideas, and finally decide how best to proceed, but now the outcome may be better!

IMPROVE ON IT

Sometimes ideas are so good that, almost on first hearing, everybody immediately recognizes that it is a great thing to do and everyone wants to get on with it. At other times, ideas get worked on for quite a period of time until finally settling on something which everyone feels is the right approach.

In both these cases, you need to pause, let a couple of days pass, then revisit the ideas and see if you can improve on them. During that intervening time the ideas tend to percolate and get thought through. When you come back and revisit them a day or two later, then a new approach, or something else that maybe wasn't thought of at the time, comes to mind and can be included. This is the process of taking an idea and trying to improve upon it before implementing it. Very often, a little energy spent in this fashion can make a really great idea brilliant, and you will receive the benefit for years to come.

Another way to improve on ideas is, once you've settled on your approach, do a little research by talking to other people who have done something similar, or get ideas from articles or organizations that have done something similar. All of these extra suggestions can allow you to improve on your original idea, and it's fun to do since the hard work is already done — coming up with the original thought.

The process of improvement is one of the more interesting and exciting aspects of organizational life. Improving ideas and suggestions is fun, exciting, and allows great room for creativity, brainstorming, and "blue sky" thinking. Initial ideas, no matter how great, can usually be improved upon with additional thought and brainstorming. Make it a priority to attempt to improve on great suggestions before their implementation. In this way, the very greatest possible benefit that can accrue to the organization will do so.

Take time to explore ways to improve on already great suggestions.

Ideas create ideas! Have fun!

PRACTICAL

*When suggesting ideas, consider whether or not
you can also help in some way to implement them.*

Once a suggestion is adopted, be part of making it come alive.

1. Many suggestions are great, and if implemented would really make a difference; often nothing happens beyond the idea because "I don't know how," or "It's hard to get started," or "It's a lot of work to do by myself," etc.

2. Help with the implementation. There are a number of ways to help:

   • Spell out in more detail how it could be done

   • Provide encouragement

   • Lend assistance – your time, energy, or resources

   • Suggest somewhere where they can get help

   • Help overcome hurdles encountered along the way

   • Reinforce the impact that will be felt once it's done ("It's worth it to make this dream a reality")

3. Sometimes a great suggestion can be discouraging to others, because it paints a picture of what could be, but the other people cannot yet see how to make it reality, even though they want to. By showing how to bring it alive, you provide not only the suggestion, but also help to achieve the impact!

PRACTICAL

A great suggestion really only has value once it's been brought to life and put into practice. Sometimes the person making the suggestion is the only one who really understands the full detail of how it can be done. The idea may be discussed, improved upon, and reworked by others, but when it comes to actually implementing it the originator may be the only one who really knows what steps to take, and so is crucial to seeing it fully realized.

Everyone may enthusiastically adopt the idea. However, you need to also be part of the implementation, and not feel that: "Well I came up with the idea, so now someone else can implement it."

If everyone participates in the implementation, then the idea has a much greater chance of coming to life. There will also be other times when implementing a suggestion you've made does not require your personal involvement, and you'll need to let it go.

Suggestions need to be practical, and they need people to help with their implementation. Once your suggestion has come forward, then the organization expects that everyone will be quick to assist with implementation. This is typically easy when the suggestion is yours, but perhaps somewhat more difficult when the suggestion is someone else's, or when yours has undergone significant transformation. Regardless, a wholehearted, enthusiastic commitment to implementation is key and is the expectation of the organization. The challenge of implementation can sometimes be as great as the challenge of the initial creation of the idea. Be part of both, as only a successful implementation of the initial idea can truly bring value.

Look to see how you can help to bring a suggestion to life.

DONE!

Be part of bringing your suggestions to life.

Conclusion

Leadership is an act of the will.

I trust you have found value within these key areas which are so crucial to success, both personally and as leaders.

Act Collaboratively: Truly understand and harness the power of teamwork.

Keep Improving Yourself: From growth comes growth. Value the importance of continually improving.

Deliver what you Promise: Accountability in ourselves, and in others, is foundational to personal success.

Maintain Balance: Think long term, not just short term, and value equilibrium.

Demonstrate Character: Who we are, what we do, how we're perceived, and how much we can accomplish are all interwoven.

Build Trust: Trust is at the very core of excellence, and without it mediocrity becomes the norm.

Get Things Done: What we do speaks far louder that what we say we'll do; so the ability to guarantee accomplishment is vital.

Make Suggestions: Being committed to helping others in a respectful way is the hallmark of a truly great leader, and so a critical skill to master.

As we strive for personal excellence each of us will, at one time or another, probably encounter challenges in one or more of these areas, either as individuals, or as leaders committed to helping others achieve greatness. How we respond to those challenges is where greatness lies; let's therefore always be mindful of the need to first lead ourselves, then lead others!